KAAN AND HER SISTERS

KAAN AND HER SISTERS
by Lena Khalaf Tuffaha

TRIO HOUSE PRESS

Copyright © July 1, 2023 Lena Khalaf Tuffaha

No part of this book may be used or preformed without written consent of the author, if living, except for critical articles or reviews.

Tuffaha, Lena Khalaf
1st edition

ISBN: 978-1-949487-14-5
Library of Congress Control Number: 2022949556

Interior design by Natasha Kane
Cover art by Sliman Mansour
Cover design by Joel W. Coggins
Editing by Halee Kirkwood and Natasha Kane

Trio House Press, Inc.
Minneapolis
www.triohousepress.org

يا حبيبي تعا تروح
قبل الوقت وقبل الحب
— فيروز

"The destruction has become the truth. It is the women who speak of the war."
—Etel Adnan

Table of Contents

Facts on the Ground / 11

Miss Sahar Tells the Story

Kaan and Her Sisters Consider the Past / 14
Upon A Time / 15
Miss Sahar Tells the Story of Spring / 16
Fashioned By Your Magic / 20
Coordinates / 21
Makaan / 23
[Interior] Bayt al Hatab / 24
Lesson: Direct Objects / 25
What Happens Next / 26

The Kingdom of Forgetting

Étude / 33
Dear Miss Sahar, *First Letter* / 34
Dear Miss Sahar, *Letter in Transit* / 36
Miss Sahar Listens to Fairuz Sing "The Bees' Path" / 37
Dear Miss Sahar, *Third Letter* / 38
Miss Sahar Listens to Fairuz Sing "I'll Write Your Name Habibi" / 39
Dear Miss Sahar, *Letter Between Translations* / 41
Miss Sahar Recites The Throne Verse / 42
Miss Sahar Completes Her Application for Travel Documents / 43
Dear Miss Sahar, *Letter After* / 47
Sings   Herself   the Rubble / 48
Dear Miss Sahar, *Letter Without Address* / 50
Kaan and Her Sisters Return / 51
Miss Sahar Listens to Fairuz Sing "Take Me" / 52

Laissez-Passez

Lemon Blossoms / 56
[Interior] Bustaan / 57
Amsa Gives the Journalists a Tour of Yarmouk / 58
Kaan and Her Sisters Survive the Siege / 59
[Interior] Namleeya / 60
Lesson: Metaphor / 61
[Interior] Khazaaneh / 62
Rootwork / 63
Baata At the Ruins / 64
Lesson: Nymphaeum / 65

Notes / 69
Acknowledgements / 73
About the Author / 75
About the Artist / 77

Facts on the Ground

After February's fallow clouds, a fraying
whip snaps the air, our bones
a winter kingdom. Silence,

our shroud, no longer softens
absence. The phone lines were always crowded
and now new frontiers for listening, for the theft

of our whispers. The unmarked van that arrives
at the end of the road is the only country
that never hesitates to take us in. Why

this particular corpse? Why this
particular death and not the many
before it, emblazoned with cigarette burns

and lacerations? What makes us think
it will be this particular boy's jaw
unlatched from his tender skull

that turns us outward, that finally wrests
the machinery of slaughter
from its masters? How many generations

of our children chasing
cameras, waving victory signs
with grimy fingers, chanting *Take*
My Picture Look
Over Here Tell
Them What Is Happening

To Us. What happened?
Our children's bodies
are infamous. The halls of foreign galleries

draped in our spectacular deaths.
Has the earth
swallowed its fill of us?

Miss Sahar Tells the Story

Kaan and Her Sisters Consider the Past

Once upon makaan they gathered,
Kaan and all the verbs that revel in negation.
What did not happen to us, what had not taken place—
these were the subjects they raised.

Kaan and her sisters were born for lamentation,
for dividing time and denying its work.
Miss Sahar taught us about this family in Arabic class,
the somber sisters of story,
and how they tell by taking time away.

Once upon makaan they walked through the market
and the woman selling grape leaves called to them
from the ground where she sat
and the girl making tea called to them
from the window of her house
and the man selling sesame loaves called to them
from his wooden cart

*Ma kaan this our homeland once upon old time? Ma kaan an end to this
    story?*

Once upon Jerusalem the boy gathering stones called out to them
Kaan a poem on this wall
but they keep trying to erase it.
I hear the words calling out to me
"If I do not burn and you do not burn
then who will light the way?"

Upon a Time

I was her student.
They were different cities then.
There was a respite between droughts
though none of us realized
our dreams, staying
or trying, always, to leave.

It is imprecise to say
that her name means magic.
A common mistranslation, though it's music—
snatched breath of its sounds—
only make dispelling
the myth more difficult.

She taught us poetry, a vessel
made of the ocean it traveled.

I remember her
telling stories, making
meaning of the arcane
rules of the classical. A living
organism, she would say
of the language and so, too, the history
she wrested from the present.

.

Miss Sahar Tells the Story of Spring

                                                  The ancestors say spring
                                      is a postman, and he and his beast
                                                    deliver the news
                                    from Damascus, Saad who left
                                        his village as the sky swelled,
                   a son named happiness. His mother did not grieve
                                  and his father said: if he slaughters,
                                                         he survives.

Happiness is land
where no one thirsts, land of roots
generations older than their caretakers.
The postman, who left his village carrying
love letters and news of trial proceedings,
walked into the certainty of hunger
and a treasonous sky. He slaughtered his beast.
His mother did not grieve.
His father said: eating the flesh of what carried him,
swallowing what housed him,
this is how Saad survived.

The ancestors knew happiness returns
with spring. A mother does not grieve
the son who leaves—even after the body
is wrapped in burial linens that temper
the open-mouthed cry, even after the procession
of men claims it for the city, ever after
young olive branches and wilting roses
follow it into the earth.
There is only ululation for our dead. A happiness
supreme is Saad returned, land
warm again, green sprouts sated. Three stars
of Denb Alguidy inaugurate this season—
Nashira glinting azure, and beneath her the Lovers.
Let your sons take their brides under these stars.
To grieve is to relinquish the child who travels.
His mother ululated.
His father said: Saad is home. Happiness
that once was returns.

The days after Supreme Happiness
determine the borders between winter and spring.
Shbaat negotiates with Athaar—three from you
and four from me, cousin, and the old woman
will have to burn her spindle to stay warm.
They are flippant, the negotiating months,
watching the women strip their cities
down to kindling. They forget that happiness
roots in language. Tyrant rains endured
yield long life or a numbness to frigid constellations.
Before the slumbering rise up
Roman days await, the strafing winds
of صن و صنبر , the deluge
of وبر, the counterfeit heat of امر و مؤتمر,
and the scorpion sting of معلل و مطفئ الجمر.
The moon eventually falls into other phases.
Our mothers miraculous, persevering.
No maps are new to the ancestors.

Fashioned by Your Magic

There are women whose work,
measure by measure, salvaging seeds,
turns night-years into staying,
as generals trade their field uniforms

for gabardine suits without ending
a single battle. The sisters sing
us our poems, whisper of becoming,
in Saba melodies of keening

skies, *our bread, our alphabet.*
They sing in Nahawand of tiled courtyards,
this is how our kohl, our blade.
In Ajam of anthems and Bayaat

of lingering mercies, *this is how
we named constellations.*
Seeka of kisses and gardenia,
this is how,

*sugared, softened. And this
is how, fasting, deserted,* Hejaz
of remembered supplication.
Raast of the minarets and Kurd

of our grandmothers' palms, *this is how
the tether, the spine.*
There are women who refuse
the scales of lullaby, lure
of new world orders, perfumes
purchased in duty-free shops
between negotiations,
women who refuse the ceremonies,

the atlases of imagined geography.

Coordinates

On our field trip we sang—as every child
of these cities does— نسم علينا الهوا, and Miss Sahar
and the bus driver swayed along to Fairuz. A war

engulfed nearby Beirut, shredding its portraits
and shipping its refugees across the Mediterranean,
but we sang, as Fairuz does,

we ate our sandwiches and sang.
At Hadrian's Arch, Miss Sahar charged ahead,
never more alive than among the stones.

On the hills, swathes of wild mustard
crowded trunks of Roumis, schoolgirls at the feet
of stately elders, speckling verdure with gold.

Miss Sahar gestured at the salvaged city,
at granite and limestone,
languid in March light. Bypassing Zeus

and his cluttered temple, heels clopping the cobblestones
of the forum, she stood in full sun
at the center of the ancient road, waved

away tour guides. The Cardo runs North-South.
Behind us, Amman. She faced the vanishing
point and said "el-Sham," our polaris

of language. I hear the pulse
of one word nesting in the womb of another,
so that when she said

"to the West, Palestine," our ancestry
was once and eternally a sunset and an estrangement.

"And to the East, Baghdad," the ق of her sharq

crackled in the parched air.
Were we ever listening, as she conjured
the wars we would endure or succumb to, the spring

that would rise up, the cities
we would march through then flee from, cities
that would bury us or let us

each one alone
watch them burn
on screens so small

we held them in our hands?

Makaan

Kaan is a verb that keeps time.
I was a song-loving child
but I've lost the rhythms of Arabic.
I used to sing *All Arab Nations Are My Homeland;*
The one that fueled a planet
The one that granted no entry visas
The one that tapped our phones
The one that sold our names for security coordination
The one where our families lived
The one where refugees waited in camps
The one where refugees slept under bridges
The one that talked tough but sang for its supper
The one that spoke in sultry tones as it ate its own
The one where you had to use the right vocabulary
The one that made men shave their beards
That one that made women cover their hair
The one where you bribe the border guards with cigarettes
The one where the border guards only took cash
The one that built palaces with people's bread
The one that made prisons of people's songs
The one that filled a desert with people's sons
The one that liked to take pictures of its excesses
The one we loved despite our wounds
and held it aloft on our broken limbs
The ones that Kaan.

[Interior] Bayt al Hatab

To store the source of what warms you
outside   to build a house for what will burn.
To keep them, kerosene and kindling—
side by side, locked behind the blue door,
and on the ledge a paper bag
of barley seeds for scattering. Because the sunbirds
hunger, too. On the roof, they sidestep carcasses
of overripe figs, their syrup summoning
ants from the tree. To keep the antidote
to the ants with the sweetness that entices them,
the tree forced to shade the structure
that will one day house its remains.

Lesson: Direct Objects

        I.   The direct object of Kaan anchors the sentence.

He had	a wife and children.
They built	a home.
Their house had	a view of the sea.
He painted	the shutters.
She planted	a garden.

        II.   Kaan's subject speaks first

Muhammad had	a wife and children.
They built	a home.
They became	*present absentees.*
Their house had	a view of the sea.
He painted	the shutters.
She planted	a garden.

        III.   Kaan is considered incomplete without its people

He had	a wife and children
Three boys, and then a girl, Sahar.	
They built	a home of Jerusalem stone.
He painted	the shutters.
She planted	a garden.

        IV.   In Kaan's sentence, the direct object is often descriptive

His heart kaan	content.
The house kaan	unassuming.
The sea kaan	glistening azure.
The shutters kaan	olive green.
To the gardenia, her touch kaan sunlight.	

What Happened Next

The timeline is teeming

Nakba unlocks the gates

                                          From our house, my father carried
                                              the suitcase and my mother
                                              carried my youngest sister.
                                                      She stopped only twice
                                                            to nurse her
                                                        then, days later,
                                                          to bury her
                                                   beneath a carob tree.

Time opens the gate

                                                   Another sister was born
                                  in the first camp where we took refuge
                                      and some parts of my mother
                                            too, though she buried
                                                her eyes on the road.

A line repeats

The Nakba is teeming with locks

                                                                  They became what they sought
                                                                      and were never granted.
                                                                         My father dissolved
                                          and my mother fed the mourning
                                                   doves. She stopped only once
                                                                            to grieve him
                                                 then, days later, she walked us
                                                                  past the snipers.

Nakba repeats itself

                                                                                 My love grew
                                 up in the second camp where we waited.
                                                              This was the era
                                                  in which we fought to return.

Let the teeming

                                                                                      My love
                                       was sent out to sea and the others—
                                                     what can I tell you?
                                The earth of the camp was too thin
                                                  to cover their corpses.

We repeat

                                                                    It always looks the same,
                                                                          lines of us walking,
                                                                                    carrying
                                                                            smaller parcels,
                                                 structures folding in on themselves

Repetition is a Nakba

                                                                                 An accord
                                                       rears its head when we meet
                                          the necessary measure of rubble.

and they took the rest of the men

in trucks through the gates

                                                                                My love has
                                                                      no address to reach us

Nakba petitions time

>My mother buried
>and, before her, my sister.
>Only once, though, if
>the first burials suffice.

The Kingdom of Forgetting

Étude

Miss Sahar always wore a pink lipstick.
Miss Sahar smoothed her green dress before she sat.
When Miss Sahar took her sandals off for prayer,
I looked to see what color she had painted her toenails.

After Miss Sahar's father died she wore only
black dresses.   Her lips were thin
and the classroom was full of the dark-roast coffee
and olive-oil-soap scent of her mourning.

Forty days later, Miss Sahar eased into midnight blue.
Sixty days later, she lined her eyes with kohl,
but her lips were still naked.   On the last Thursday of school,
Miss Sahar wore her green dress again.

The teachers whispered about a prisoner exchange
and brought date cookies on a silver tray.
Miss Sahar was dancing in the teachers' lounge.
The drumbeat beckoning me from the playground,

I squinted to see through the keyhole.
There she was: green dress hiked up
her dimpled thighs, floral scarf knotted
around her hips, her arm tracing soft curves

across the sky. There they were:
the religion teacher with her soft belly,
the math teacher with the 's' shaped scar on her forehead,
the geography teacher with her cigarette breath,
and Miss Sahar, swaying
together, rose corals
in a sea of song.

Dear Miss Sahar
First Letter

Everyone is gathered in the square
and the square is a center that cannot hold,
and the center is alive and burning.

I don't know when it happened and yet
I've known it since you taught us the first lines
of the poems we sang. Now

I understand they were a compass.
In the small country of our high school classroom
we didn't know we were afraid.

The architecture of our cities
is designed to house the fearful.
Now having lived in the heart

and on the margins, maybe
we've reached the end
of fear, our bones broken so often

they've set it new shapes. Maybe
we are finally free
of our predestinations. Everyone is in the square,

Miss Sahar, and the streets ache for their names.
We're taking long drags of tear gas
when it's fired into our midst.

I used to think this only happened
when the soldiers spoke other languages,
but I've been cured of that condition.

Our lungs are being decolonized
or incinerated, I can't tell. The sound

of singing and the scarcity of sleep

are making me light-headed, reordering the rules
of language. Yesterday a groom carried his bride
through the square, slender vine of Damascus jasmine.

A people's wedding, the joyous rave
at the end of sorrow. Everywhere
is liberation and chanting

threaded with gunfire. The girls have flowers
in their hair, Miss Sahar, and the boys are sharing
their cigarettes. There is suddenly bread

enough for all of us
or do we hunger or something more?
The time for Kaan is setting, Miss Sahar,

I need a new grammar for this country.

Dear Miss Sahar
Letter In Transit

We have to leave. We have
left. We are made to. We continue
to leave. We're luckier

than most, but can't carry much
of what I love. What called us
out of stony sleep and into the streets

seems imagined now. I thought it mattered
that we were present when, for speaking,
death hunted us. I'm not sure

where we'll end up, only that we're leaving,
that among the little I've made room for
is a notebook filled with sentence diagrams

and the marginalia of childhood,
sununus I sketched in your classes,
the dream-palace of days when I lived

in the shelter of a mother-tongue.

Miss Sahar Listens to Fairuz Sing "The Bees' Path"

If you're going to go,
if you're going to scorch this heart
and leave a desert in your absence,
tell me now and I'll follow the bees.

If you're going to scorch this heart,
I'll hem the horizon in solitude.
Tell me now and I'll follow the bees
inside the anemones scarring the hillside.

I'll hem the horizon in solitude,
the light lengthening, breaking
inside the anemones scarring the hillside.
I'll spiral beneath the dome of the sky.

The light lengthening, breaking
this moment gathered around us
as I spiral inside the dome of the sky.
Spring is a ravishment forever dying dying dying.

This moment gathered around us is
honey and wild greens and the promise
of ravishment forever dying dying dying.
We're just another love song, remembered or forgotten.

Honey and wild greens and the promise
of losing you in the desert of what happens next.
We're just another love song, remembered or forgotten.
Will you stay until the anemones fold back into the land?

Will you stay until the anemones fold back into the land
or leave a desert in your absence?
Are we just another love song, remembered or forgotten?
Tell me now and I'll follow the bees.

Dear Miss Sahar
Third Letter

Maybe a child
should be burdened with a dream at birth.
We named her Ayda.

At first, I didn't want to,
thinking it too heavy a burden for a new life,
but I thought better when within a few hours
we had to fill out the paperwork that asked us
to locate her in the world.

Maybe a dream stays the blood-dimmed tide,
straightens the spine, roots a language inside the throat.
We gave her a map that no one here recognizes.

At first, I didn't want to,
I thought it too heavy a coat for a young heart,
but I thought better of it within a few years,
and her shoulders grew stronger
under the map she had to wear in the world.

Maybe a child should be given a map for her journey.
Maybe a map protects against
a history hurtling into the future.

Miss Sahar Listens to Fairuz Sing "I'll Write Your Name Habibi"

I gathered the letters of your name
the day they came for you.
It is not our custom to cry
when what is needed is fortitude.

The day they came for you
I strung my tears like pearls on silk thread
when what is needed is fortitude.
I worried the letters of your name like prayer beads.

I strung my tears like pearls on silk thread
to withstand your absence, the weight of days.
I worried the letters of your name like prayer beads,
clasped them on my wrists like shackles

to withstand your absence, the weight of days.
You scattered the letters of my name and I
clasped yours on my wrists like shackles,
embrace of cold silver, bracelet of light.

You scattered the letters of my name and I
etched the letters of yours into the olive,
embrace of cold silver, bracelet of light, I
slid them, like globes of sap, beneath its bark, I

etched the letters of your name into the olive,
silent knife-edged prayer, alphabet incantation. I
slid them, globes of sap, beneath its bark
to nourish you with the pulse of our waiting.

Silent, knife-edged prayer, alphabet incantation,
when rains course over the wounds of this story
to nourish you with the pulse of our waiting,
your name will burn in night lanterns.

When rains course over the wounds of this story
your name will shelter beneath olive leaves,
your name will burn in night lanterns
as we carry our bodies across another border.

Your name will shelter beneath olive leaves.
It is not our custom to cry
as we carry our bodies. Across another border,
I gathered the letters of your name.

Dear Miss Sahar
Letter Between Translations

We argue about how to say
where we're going. Home

is the only translation
I can accept. She counters that the word

I use transliterates to Country.
I hear your words in my own *That way of thinking*

*is how we survived
the British and the French and before them,*

the Ottomans and since them a list long and knotted.
Though she distrusts nations, she concedes my word

 is how we might yet survive.

She's always teasing me about the signatures
of an empire in my pronunciation.

I'm waiting for her to notice
the younger one speaking through her.

Miss Sahar Recites the Throne Verse

Because the sound of what is read
is born in the dim recesses of the throat
that share a space with aleph
as it parts our lips for breath

The Living, the Ever-Wakeful

Because it is applied to our heads like
a gauze bandage to mitigate the blows
of sleepless wandering

No drowsiness distracts Him, no slumber

Because a mother whispers
it first, and calls us back
to our first homeland, to safe waters.

His throne encompasses the heavens and the earth

Because it is a learned reflex and
verse spills out of us when the wound
is open, when the raft threatens
to capsize, when the stillness
of the stars that witness it all
needs shattering.

Miss Sahar Completes Her Application for Travel Documents

1. You must take with you at least two days' rations

I often find myself in this predicament,
my mouth crowded with farewells. One letter
dropped for another, from system of meaning
to nonsense. And in this manner, we upend
the drudgery of time-telling.

I have nothing
to show for my survival.
I arrive at the precise moment
of spectacle. My father who died waiting
did not wish to repeat the story
of the almonds ripening on the tree,
of stepping beyond the threshold
of the house first, because my mother could not,
or of the clap of her palms
against her thobe, bewildered
by the task of choosing what little to carry.

2. You must have sufficient money for your onward journey

There is a word for this, the clatter
of a life disassembling, prayers
passing between the already dead
and the dying who must bury them.
In the camp, our purpose is to survive
thirst and rations and waiting
on the verge.

3. You must see that your travel document is filled out completely

Prayer for the Dead:
Blessed be those who are buried in their homeland
Prayer for Those Who Might Yet Die:

Blessed be those who carry the keys to their homes wrapped in linens.
Prayer for the Dying Burying Their Dead:
Blessed be those who do not outlive their children.
Prayer for Its Own Sake:
Spare us any more of these blessings.

4. **If any of your party are over twelve years of age, they must have a separate document with their photo on it**

I tell the students, if you forego
the diacritic marks, one hundred
can sound like death or like water.
These papers claim us
for no one but the crossing.
The beginning and the end
will be no different.

5. **You are not allowed to carry gold**

In the camp, I learned an alphabet
for singing. The women who taught us
were younger than our mothers,
and we aged together. Our rations
were flour and oil and the poems
stitched into the linings
of our uniforms. Bite down on these verses,
they will not tarnish. Weigh them
at the jeweler's shop in the city.
A people cannot survive on bread
and gunpowder alone.

6. **You are not allowed to carry any letters for persons residing outside Palestine.**

Letter to the Interior:

They have always known our name.

7. **Your baggage may not exceed sixty kilos**

> I want nothing from this holding station.
> My mother left
> the kettle on the stove. There is
> a lemon tree, she tells me, behind the window
> and always mint in the garden.
> Every road in our village will be
> wide enough for us to walk side by side.
> What could I need
> that is not already there?

8. **You must report to the nearest police office within twenty four hours of arrival at destination**

Where were you born

                                        Do you speak the language

Where was your father born
What is your father's name
What is your grandfather's name
What is his father

                                                  Are you now

Where was your mother

                                      Or have you ever been

Where is it on a map

                                    nostalgic for their childhood

Do you have anything to declare
Do you have anything left to lose
Did you consider the implications of

                                          continuing to survive

Do you recognize the state of

                                      affairs that keep you here

Do you know the number of

                gates you will have to be granted passage through
Do you believe in

                                        an ending
Do you know the location of your village
Did you pack your own

                            onions for the tear gas
Do you recognize any of these

                                    lost battles

How long do you plan to stay
Can you enunciate
Can you write

            the names and addresses of everyone you know here

Do you understand the laws

                    that make all your responses a provocation

Dear Miss Sahar
Letter After

I won't enumerate again the things
I've let go to survive. I dreamt that I could not speak, a fall
from language. Such paltry songs are made of our sorrows. Apart
from our own names, too unknown to be grieved, the
losses are vast enough to become invisible. Center-
screen, unrecognized in cycles of disaster, we cannot
break free. Next, a morality play takes hold:
how we've made our own destruction inevitable. The mere
mention of our living translates as a call to anarchy.
I dream this drowning and it is
now our daily bread. Each day, empire's hunger is loosed
upon us. I won't summon the vocabulary when called upon
to explain or historicize myself. May the
words never return. Without them, let me re-enter world.

Sings   Herself   The Rubble

I   my   land

Tomorrow   end   my poem.
Will I see you   ,   ?
          when you return?

         war   and   my poem.

                  young departing.

      you   return?

            your name a home.

         this language   uncountried

I have   your name

      a   this drought.

language   , alone   my heart

leaves   stranger, no one

                beneath us hunger
No one   is mine.

                     words
the
     earth   hungers for our limbs.

           remain here,   ?

                salvage   un

        there, peaceful, victorious?
Tomorrow   will end

                                        morning
                            o land.

Dear Miss Sahar
Letter Without Address

I don't know if I should leave a record
of my voice or where to send a message.
My need for reassurance shames me; now
more burden than care. I'm uncertain of
the last place you landed. What little I knew
of your troubles, my sight obscured by expanses
of ruin. Scrolling through satellite maps,

I scan for building numbers, Abu Akram's
grocery store, his plastic lawn chair, the hand-
lettered sign above the door. This searching,
this wait, the work your eyes have done for years.
I pray names of street trees: Let acacia
be standing. Let linden and rosewood and
red juniper. Please, if you can, call me.

Kaan and Her Sisters Return

Kaan looks over her shoulder, tastes salt
on her tongue, recognizes the fragrance of oranges.
She circles the city, bride of the sea,

in search of streets renamed. Strands of tulle
frayed, yellowing, drift from the citrus trees.
In a hairline crack in the wall, pearl

seeds, glinting in the light. Kaan
and her sisters ask about the old tailor's shop,
the bakery, the painter's loft above the fractured waves.

Fish fry in rancid oil where once upon
this place a saint intoned a seaside supplication.
They are not aesthetic choices—the domed roof

above this restaurant, the charming, the cobblestone,
the archway—they are not artifacts. The foundations
of stolen houses. The shorelines

clothed in wisps of cloud. Kaan stumbles
upon her dinner plates at an antique shop.
Saar notices her laundry suspended

from the ceiling of an art gallery. How to write
this story of unhoused objects
and their owners, of inside-out words? Mouthless,

museumed, some of the homes still stand. At the site
of departure, the waves. Kaan touches
the earth, listens for the rustle of wedding silk.

Saar stands alongside her, insists
we are not salt, have not dissolved.

Miss Sahar Listens to Fairuz Sing "Take Me"

Take me to a house with no doors.
Let the wind carry us, Habibi,
to a country of windows framing the waves,
and leave me on the balcony of the sea.

Let the wind carry us, Habibi,
return us to the days we lived there,
in our country of windows framing the waves,
before our loves departed without farewells.

Return us to the days we lived there,
to a mawaal in the orchard,
before our loves departed without farewells
to wait in the kingdom of forgetting.

Mawaal in the orchard,
lemon blossoms falling from fingers,
I wait for you in the kingdom of forgetting
Habibi, I listen for the echo of your song

and lemon blossoms fall from my fingers.
Take me to a house with no doors,
to a country of windows framing the waves.
I wait for you in the kingdom of forgetting.

Laissez-Passez

Lemon Blossoms

In Miss Sahar's class we learned
to conjugate the verb Saar,
a variant of the past tense.

We learned that to describe what became of the people
we would have to remember
a tray of cheese pastries supple
and pale, nestled in neat rows.

We would have to remember the people
who knead the cheese and semolina
into dough, silken yards
stretched into pliant tenderness by their hands.

We would have to remember the people
who harvest Aleppo pistachios and with their thumbnails
slit the skin of the fruit down to the bone-white shell,
excise the nut and crush it to powder.

We would have to remember the people
who gather lemon blossoms in winter, bathe petals
in syrup and ease them over a quiet flame,
transforming the buds into a garnet-colored jam.

We would have to remember the people
who make the cheese pastries stuffed with sweetened cream,
pistachios now a dust the color of hillsides
in spring, the lemon blossoms a blood-bright garnish,

the people now besieged, eating weeds
and sipping soiled snow that pools
in craters of rubble throughout the camp.
This is how we learned to conjugate Saar.

[Interior] Bustaan

To beguile, to line the rim
with geranium flourishes, the artifice
of abundance. This is the home-
land, interior where songbirds bathe in a modest fountain,
where a woman loosens her scarf and sips
her afternoon coffee. Here the lemon tree
aglow, benevolent, and the grapevine
readying its leaves for folding. As distinguished
from strata of olive roots, their families a foundation
for our cities, a trellis for generations of departed. As distinguished
from the wastelands of welcome where the rosemary
waves elegant fingers. Here, on slender bracts, in circles
nesting in a succession of squares, an infinity
of evenings unfold like reticent gardenia,
like threadbare jasmine vines bursting with stars.

Amsa Gives the Journalists a Tour of Yarmouk

You will write about us: the remnants—remarkable.
      The moment suspends meaning
           and requires no nameplates.

You've been here before, with cameras and questions,
      this time, a better signal, a richer image.
           Of our severed and blood-stained, stories

are fashioned. On our bones, the breaking
      news cycle feeds. I know you, guests of the aftermath,
         come to speak on inevitability.

What can you recite of the archive?
        How many times, while we wait,
            must we die?

How far back will you look to discern
      if this moment is mean or variance? Who among us
         will deviate from our given value?

You have arrived to survey,
     and our bodies are best used
         to express an average.

Let the lines of us, the laissez-passers
      unfolded for inspection, lead the evening
          headlines. Let the pianist play a soundtrack

of these days. None of this will draw blood.
      Behind the screen, none will drown for knowing.
         Let this gathering, then,

leave us.
       Let evening fall on us,
           your monuments.

Kaan and Her Sisters Survive the Siege

It began in their youth,
so Kaan and her sisters were raised
to subsist on little. In each of them
a hunger throbbed,

dull and dependable. Bread grew thinner
than paper. In winter, they were lucky.
They could burn their notebooks
and stir water with long spoons over the flames.

A dash of salt, the last few grains of cumin,
                              the prayer of it,
watching this liar's broth boil over a history
incinerating. Then water ran out.

They were unlucky in summer. The flavors
of bygone meals evaporated, the sky's pallid glare
blistered their skin, driving them underground.
The roots and leaves of spring long shriveled,

Kaan and her sisters foraged for geranium ghosts,
fought the last of the sparrows for crumbs.
When no help arrived, they remembered
that their heritage made them ineligible

for mourning. They surrendered their mouths
and ate the air, chewing through its smoldering
fibers, losing teeth to shrapnel
and shards of language.

[Interior] Namleeya

To name a place by what it keeps
out   what it wards off
to name your sanctuary after what can consume it
to live on the edge of a growing desert
and water with abiding faithfulness the apricot trees
the midnight-skinned eggplants

To take what is sour and let it smolder
in sugar   in flames
to loosen the alchemy of sun and time
at its heart
to stave off winter in jar after jar
of what light has made
what your hands gathered

To hold the ravenous march at bay
in the shade of a quiet cabinet
to remember that even in its name
stone harbors some
of the damp alphabet of ocean

Lesson: Metaphor

                                                    In the desert of the imagination
                                      a mythology readies to be born. Returning
                                            and returning to the footpaths
                                                      of worn texts, the cities
In 1919 we weren't afraid
to say what we knew to be true
of an emperor, to write it on the walls

                            swell with bodies, laborer and lettered,
                            hope unrepentant is loosed upon the land.
we declared
an Arab republic at the river's mouth
and rose unfettered by imported bombs and fatwas.

                                      but the ceremony of freedom
                                        is always drowned. The city
                            dwellers leave their kettles on the stove,
                              the farmers sow no forage for their beasts.
                        single-minded and pitiless as the sun, an empire
                                        prepares its peace plans.
in Filastin, in Surya, we
were part of the world becoming.

                            Where we live, Bethlehem is no metaphor.
                                We cradle our children in our arms.

[Interior] Khazaaneh

Unlocked, the wardrobe revealed her own map of the world,
daughters and sons in mandatory grisaille
with scallop-edged frames, pinned inside,
their glistening coiffes and pencil-thin eyebrows
a constellation above the altar
of perfumes and medicine bottles.

A passport was the possibility
of farewells, of funerals. Between Asr prayer
and evening's veil of crinoline,
the children who could assembled
and interlaced their own breath,
a net for her last. Later, lifting her

body overhead on the first steps
of her last journey, some of them chanted
with shaking voices about God,
that He remains, though it was muscle memory,
her own practice repeated was their final
offering. Inside her wardrobe,
they were granted residence.

Rootwork

In Arabic class we learned that all words
can be traced back to their three-letter roots.
Miss Sahar used to slash through their hearts

with chalk to show us. The distance between *a writer* and *her desk*
or *the one* and *loneliness*
were coiled in the majuscules of ء

lurking in ا's languid yawn.
When words form a dense fog, I go foraging. It's easiest
with the news. That vocabulary shrinks year after year.

I know the few letters needed for understanding.
In our language, the difference between *witness* and *tombstone*

is just one vowel.

Baata at the Ruins

At the doorstep, the sea
is strangely visible. Stripped
of the memories she carried,
Baata must navigate a world without structures.

The village reveals itself in shards
and she extracts them
from her grandmother's sentences—the flesh
in which they were lodged tender, aflame.

Carob trees beside the old post office,
a graveyard crowning the hillside, the salt air
layered in crisp sheets beneath afternoon sun.
A public park, a beautified absence,

at first glance, seems a lesser wound
than an asylum at the site of massacre.
On the phone, her grandmother's voice
peoples the stretch of land before her,

naming the residents of the graves
whose headstones have been defaced,
counting paces to vanished balconies.
The house shelters day

—dreaming, the house protects
the dreamer. Baata is wide awake
on the lip of a homeland shorn of its dreamers,
wild anemones blazing,

siren threads in uninhabited fields.

Lesson: Nymphaeum

                          Whatever you do,
                                 resist
               our monuments. Think instead
          of the hands that were made to build them.
            Through fissures in stone walls,
             primaveral thistle finds a path,
         blue-violet in April, delicate Canaanite
                    banners. There will be talk
             of crisis, of urgency, but water
            has always been scarce. We live
               where we trust it runs, where
              it returns. Leaves, once supple
           and quenched, harden into spears.

Kaan and her sisters, Saar, Baata, Ma Zaal—
what was and what became and what remains—
are verbs for phases of drought.

              Like thorns, we remain, as the poet
               declaimed. They've harvested our names
            and lifted the land beneath our houses.
        They are renovating the ancient temple where,
             before we knew God, we prayed
                 for rain. They love nothing
                    like a history denuded,
            reprinted for postcards. The past
              tense is incomplete. It wants
            and we answer: Tomorrow!
             We answer tomorrow with
               today's shackled hands.

Notes

Nakba-n., Arabic, *Catastrophe,* the name given to the destruction of the Palestinian homeland in 1948 and the culminating exile of over 800,000 Palestinians, many of whom still live in 58 refugee camps throughout the Arab world today, in cities including Amman, Damascus, and Beirut. The worldwide Palestinian refugee population numbers 7.2 million.

Kaan- v., *was,* **Saar**-v., *became,* **Ma Zaal** v.,-*remained* and their sister verbs including **Amsa, Baata**. In Arabic grammar, these past tense verbs are described as a sisterhood. The past tense verbs inflect their subjects, changing their sounds and spelling on the page.

Saad-n., Happiness, proper noun, *m.*
In the Arab homelands of the Eastern Mediterranean, a shared heritage thrives. I came upon the folkloric tale of Saad in fragments and idioms, relayed by Palestinian elders. The story maps the weather patterns of late winter and early spring, and each Saad corresponds to a phase of the moon and its attendant agricultural and culinary practices.

Shbaat, Athaar—*February, March* in Palestinian and Levantine Arabic.

Fairuz-n., the best known living singer in the Arab world, born Nouhad Haddad, in Lebanon. Her songs constitute the morning soundtrack on radio stations in Arab cities East and West. Each of the "Miss Sahar Listens to Fairuz Sing" poems borrows a title from one of her songs, and all are a written after the lyrics of the Rahbani brothers.

Sabra, Shatila, Tal Zaatar, and Yarmouk—Palestinian refugee camps in Lebanon and Syria, built after the initial Nakba of 1948. Each has become an island of exile in the heart of an Arab city, each the site of infamous sieges and massacres of their residents.

Namleeya, Bayt Al Hatab, Bustaan, Khazaaneh—*Pantry, Woodshed, Garden,* and *Wardrobe* respectively.

Epigraph—Etel Adnan, *Of Cities & Women (Letters to Fawwaz)*.

DEAR MISS SAHAR, LESSON: METAPHOR
In a pattern not dissimilar to the revolutions in Arab cities during 2011, a wave of resistance marked the spring of 1919. Cities in Palestine and Syria and other Arab homelands rose up to confront European colonialism. It was also the year that W.B. Yeats wrote the poem "The Second Coming." Each of the DEAR MISS SAHAR letters borrows a line from Yeats' poem; "Dear Miss Sahar, *Letter After*" is a golden shovel after the Yeats poem, and "Lesson: Metaphor" reimagines it entirely, looking back on 1919 from the Arab Spring revolutions of 2011.

FASHIONED BY YOUR MAGIC
The line "imagined geography" comes from Edward Said's collection *After the Last Sky*.
Fashioned By Your Magic, صنع بسحرك, is a mnemonic device to remember the names of the eight maqamaat, the melodic scales of Arabic music.

WHAT HAPPENED NEXT
"They took the rest of the men in trucks through the gate" is my translation of the testimony of a Palestinian survivor of Sabra and Shatila massacre, from an interview about her experience on the BBC Arabic program Al-Mashhad.

SINGS HERSELF THE RUBBLE
The line "will I see you there, peaceful, victorious?" comes from Ibrahim Touqan's poem "Mawtini", written during the anti-colonial revolutions of the 1930s, and adopted as a Palestinian anthem.

KAAN AND HER SISTERS
The line "If I do not burn, and you do not burn, then who will light the way?" comes from Nazem Hikmet's "Like Karem."

AMSA GIVES THE JOURNALISTS A TOUR OF THE CAMP
Ayham Ahmed became the "Pianist of Yarmouk" during the siege of the camp in Damascus in the winter of 2012-13.

BAATA AT THE RUINS
The line "the house shelters daydreaming, the house shelters the

dreamer." comes from Gaston Bachelard's *The Poetics of Space*.

There are many references, living and remembered, whose songs, stories, and journeys demanded this telling. Most of all, my Arabic teachers: Nu'om Husni Fariz, who first transformed language into story with her drawings of ل sitting on a park bench. Sahar, uncompromising, Damascene. Asmaa Jaafar, who dried my tears when I didn't want to move to the US, showed me the poetry of the mahjar, and said "write to us." Rabeeha Abu Qura, who said that elegy is a native love song and a liberatory act. The late Paulette Shamieh, who first gave me permission. The late Hayat Hwayyek, who showed me that women remake language. Terri DeYoung, who nurtured my Fairouz-songs-as-portal obsession.

Acknowledgments

Grateful acknowledgment to Diode Editions for publishing several of these poems in the chapbook *Letters from the Interior*, and to the following journals for first publishing these poems, sometimes in slightly different forms:

Adroit: "Lesson: Nymphaeum," "Miss Sahar Tells the Story of Spring"
Alaska Quarterly Review: "Kaan and Her Sisters Survive the Siege"
Barrow Street: "Makaan"
Bird's Thumb: "Miss Sahar Listens to Fairuz Sing 'I'll Write Your Name Habibi,'" "Miss Sahar Recites The Throne Verse"
Black Warrior Review: "Dear Miss Sahar/First Letter"
The Boiler: "[Interior] Namleeya"
Diode: "Lemon Blossoms"
Drunken Boat: "Étude" (published as "Private Lessons")
Greensboro Review: "Miss Sahar Listens to Fairuz Sing 'The Bees' Way,'" winner of the 2019 Robert Watson Literary Prize
Hermeneutic Chaos: "Dear Miss Sahar/Third Letter"
Hypertext: "Dear Miss Sahar/Letter in Translation"
Ithaca Lit: "Kaan and Her Sisters Consider the Past"
Jubilat: "Coordinates"
Moria: "Miss Sahar Listens to Fairuz Sing 'Take Me'"
Michigan Quarterly Review: "Lesson: Direct Objects," "Kaan and Her Sisters Return"
The Normal School: "   Sings   Herself   the Rubble"
Pittsburgh Poetry Review: "Rootwork"
Southern Humanities Review: "Facts on the Ground"
West Branch: "Amsa Gives the Journalists a Tour of Yarmouk"

About the Author

Lena Khalaf Tuffaha is a poet, essayist, and translator. Her work has appeared in *the Nation*, *New England Review*, *Michigan Quarterly Review*, *Poetry Northwest*, and *Southern Humanities Review*. Her debut collection of poems, *Water & Salt*, won the 2018 Washington State Book Award and was a finalist for the Arab American Book Award. She lives in Redmond, Washington with her family.

About the Artist

Al-Quds-based artist Sliman Mansour was born in 1947 in Birzeit. He is one of the most distinguished and renowned artists in Palestine. His work has been exhibited internationally in cities including Gaza, Cairo, Amman, Sharjah, Paris, London, and New York City. His work has received numerous awards including the 2019 UNESCO-Sharjah Prize for Arab Culture.

Thanks

The earliest draft of the first of these poems was written in Meadow cottage at Hedgebrook in April 2015. For the time, care, community, and lilacs of that space, I am forever grateful.

Early drafts of this manuscript benefited from conversations with my Rainier Writing Workshop mentors, especially Oliver De La Paz and Lia Purpura.

Heartfelt gratitude to Aracelis Girmay, Molly Spencer, and Solmaz Sharif, whose questions and wisdom are sustenance.

To Naseem—every love song.

About the Book

Kaan and Her Sisters was designed at Trio House Press through the collaboration of:

Halee Kirkwood, Lead Editor
Natasha Kane, Supporting Editor and Interior Design
Joel W. Coggins, Cover Design
Sliman Mansour, Cover Art

The text is set in Adobe Caslon Pro.

The publication of this book is made possible, whole or in part, by the generous support of the following individuals or agencies:

Anonymous

About the Press

Trio House Press is an independent literary press publishing three or more collections of poems annually. Our mission is to promote poetry as a literary art enhancing culture and the human experience. We offer two annual poetry awards: the Trio Award for First of Second Book for emerging poets, and the Louise Bogan Award for Artistic Merit and Excellence for a book of poems contributing in an innovative and distinct way to American poetry. All manuscripts submitted to the annual contests are considered for publication.

Trio House Press adheres to and supports all ethical standards and guidelines outlined by the CLMP.

Trio House Press, Inc. is dedicated to the promotion of poetry as literary art, which enhances the human experience and its culture. We contribute in an innovative and distinct way to poetry by publishing emerging and established poets, providing educational materials, and fostering the artistic process of writing poetry. For further information, or to consider making a donation to Trio House Press, please visit us online at www.triohousepress.org.

Other Trio House Press books you might enjoy:

States of Arousal by Sunshine O'Donnell / 2023 Louise Bogan Award Winner selected by Ed Bok Lee

The Fight by Jennifer Manthey / 2023 Trio Award Winner selected by Aileen Cassinetto

Live in Suspense by David Groff / 2023

A Northern Spring by Matt Mauch / 2023

Bloomer by Jessica Hincapie / 2022 Louise Bogan Award Winner selected by Lee Ann Roripaugh

The Fallow by Megan Neville / 2022 Trio Award Winner selected by Steve Healey

The Traditional Feel of the Ballroom by Hannah Rebecca Gamble / 2021

Third Winter in Our Second Country by Andres Rojas / 2021

Sweet Beast by Gabriella R. Tallmadge / 2020 Louise Bogan Award Winner selected by Sandy Longhorn

Songbox by Kirk Wilson / 2020 Trio Award Winner selected by Malena Mörling

YOU DO NOT HAVE TO BE GOOD by Madeleine Barnes / 2020

X-Rays and Other Landscapes by Kyle McCord / 2019

Threed, This Road Not Damascus by Tamara J. Madison / 2019

My Afmerica by Artress Bethany White / 2018 Trio Award Winner selected by Sun Yung Shin

Waiting for the Wreck to Burn by Michele Battiste / 2018 Louise Bogan Award Winner selected by Jeff Friedman

Cleave by Pamel Johnson Parker / 2018 Trio Award Winner selected by Jennifer Barber

Two Towns Over by Darren C. Demaree / 2018 Louise Bogan Award Winner selected by Campbell McGrath

Bird~Brain by Matt Mauch / 2017

Dark Tussock Moth by Mary Cisper / 2016 Trio Award Winner selected by Bhisham Bherwani

The Short Drive Home by Joe Osterhaus / 2016 Louise Bogan Award Winner selected by Chard DeNiord

Break the Habit by Tara Betts / 2016

Bone Music by Stephen Cramer / 2015 Louise Bogan Award Winner selected by Kimiko Hahn

Rigging a Chevy into a Time Machine and Other Ways to Escape a Plague by Carolyn Hembree / 2015 Trio Award Winner selected by Neil Shepard

Magpies in the Valley of Oleanders by Kyle McCord / 2015

Your Immaculate Heart by Annmarie O'Connell / 2015

The Alchemy of My Mortal Form by Sandy Longhorn / 2014 Louise Bogan Award Winner selected by Peter Campion

What the Night Numbered by Bradford Tice / 2014 Trio Award Winner selected by Carol Frost

Flight of August by Lawrence Eby / 2013 Louise Bogan Award Winner selected by Joan Houlihan

The Consolations by John W. Evans / 2013 Trio Award Winner selected by Mihaela Moscaliuc

Fellow Odd Fellow by Stephen Riel / 2013

Clay by David Groff / 2012 Louise Bogan Award Winner selected by Michael Waters

Gold Passage by Iris Jamahl Dunkle / 2012 Trio Award Winner selected by Ross Gay

If You're Lucky Is a Theory of Mine by Matt Mauch / 2012